Illustrated by El Davo

To Olive,
Thanks for opening my heart.
Dad
X

Praise for Todd's original book, *Own Life*

Dan Richards
The Best Book I have Ever Set Eyes On
I've just got to Chapter 3 and I can officially say (with tears in my eyes, that's how good it is!) that this is the best book I have ever set eyes on. That is because it's not just another self-help book, it's more like an EXAM of your life, LITERALLY.

It's mind blowing! and I have also not stopped writing, as he states to 'pick up your pen and write' and I've never felt so indulged to do so, because he wants to you really go in depth and explore your life and what he is asking of you.
I have found it simply INCREDIBLE, that I couldn't help but do an early review which I never normally tend to do but I have been mind-blown by this book, and I feel by the end of it (as just by flicking through, you can see lots of 'reflect and write' scattered throughout the book) I could become a completely different person! this is what is so mesmerising.

R. Bajic
Want to Know Yourself?
A very easy read and takes what most people consider the difficult parts of their lives or confusing parts and breaks it down to understand yourself. There is no right or wrong in your life in this book. Just tries to lay it out so you can better understand yourself and what you want in life, what you want to achieve or just self-understanding of who you are. But in doing so you sort of get to understand others in your life too and how they are. The illustrations are brilliant too and help resonate the points the book is explaining.

David Robertson

This book is so good that I want to keep putting it down. Todd Eden has succeeded in creating a book on personal development that is genuinely and profoundly thought-provoking. Right from the start, the questions, and exercises grabbed my attention and had me putting the book down to think and reflect. I have always a very occasional journaler, but since reading Own Life I have been loving finding quiet moments throughout the day to focus on the bigger questions. The book is both practical and energising. It helps you to reflect on what really matters to you, but then it helps you to put in place practical and actionable strategies to help you take control of your life. I love it.

Todd has taught thousands of delegates around the world, and after completing the course, each one is asked, 'What will you do differently now?'

Here follows a selection of their responses, which all start with

"I will…"

'… achieve my goals whatever it may take.' [Charidimos V]
'… be much more confident.' [Hadra A]
'… be more confident talking to new people.' [Elizabeth G]
'… be more grateful about being myself.' [Mohamad A]
'… be a better version of myself.' [Nicole E]
'… believe in myself.' [Maddi M]
'… change.' [Alex M]
'… achieve my potential.' [Abdulla R]
'… be more productive.' [Fahmid C]
'… feel comfortable being myself to others.' [Elissar B]
'… be more resilient to the voices in my head.' [Natasha J]
'… be more aware of the potential that I have.' [Emine O]
'… start improving my habits and focus on priorities.' [Marta M]
'… be more interactive with others.' [Dongho L]
'… manage my problems well.' [Umar T]
'… be more open.' [Marta O]
'… handle setbacks better.' [Rosemary C]
'… stop coming up with excuses.' [Javor G]
'… be more positive.' [Mathilda C]
'… be more motivated to achieve my goals.' [Iva K]
'… strive to better my self-discipline.' [Sean M]
'… step out of my comfort zone.' [Margherita C]
'… be more organized.' [Abdul R]
'… have more purpose in everything I do.' [Luksa K]

'... be more committed towards my goals.' [Mohamed A]

'... be more productive.' [Sharon S]

'... face my fears.' [Tanu C]

'... be more confident in myself.' [Madalina M]

'... have purpose in my actions.' [Louise M]

'... face the tasks that I avoid because of fear.' [James W]

'... step out of my comfort zone.' [Daniela B]

'... start changing unhealthy habits.' [Augustin L]

'... set goals for myself.' [Nilay S]

'... pursue my goals.' [Jeremiah U]

'... implement mindfulness.' [Lauren C]

'... be an active listener.' [Anira B]

'... set my goals.' [Imani S]

'... know myself better.' [Abhishek B]

'... not be afraid to share my thoughts with others.' [Disha S]

'... make the most of what I have.' [Tiffany D]

'... be more authentic.' [Ellarene C]

'... accept myself.' [Alice V]

'... apply for jobs I was unsure about.' [Marco A]

'... believe in my ability.' [Hannah S]

'... be more confident in myself.' [Amy F]

'... appreciate different opinions.' [Ana M]

'... work harder towards my goals.' [Andres G]

'... face my future strong.' [Arjunan R]

'... commit with purpose.' [Camilo R]

'... push myself to leave my comfort zone.' [Daniel C]

'... keep improving myself.' [Emmanuel O]

'... control my inner voice.' [Hiren T]

'... be a better leader.' [Ieva G]

'... adopt mindfulness and talk to strangers.' [James T]

'... feel more confident around people.' [Jessica F]

'... be more self-aware.' [Kabilas P]

'... feel more confident to apply for certain jobs.' [Katherine H]

'... put myself in the shoes of others more often.' [Kilian B]

'... take responsibility for my life.' [Lanja R]

'... take risks.' [Lauren M]

'... get out of my comfort zone.' [Madhumitha K]

'... listen more.' [Michal C]

'... be more confident.' [Nantia B]

'... have more confidence in myself.' [Polly S]

'... be more mindful.' [Rosie G]

'... be more ready to take the lead.' [Samuel S]

'... be more introspective.' [Sian W]

'... take better care of my health.' [Sushma S]

'... always say positive things about myself.' [Toyyibat B]

'... be more resilient.' [Yakubu S]

'... be willing to step out of my comfort zone.' [Sabrina C]

'... continue to be me.' [Samantha C]

'... make a difference.' [Debbie F]

'... believe in myself more.' [Manvinder D]

'... express myself better.' [Hasit G]

'... be kinder to myself.' [Jad J]

'... trust other people more.' [Ashley A]

'... stop trying to solve other people's problems.' [Brandon M]

'... be more understanding.' [Noi B]

By the end of this book, what will you be doing?

CONTENTS

HOW TO THRIVE ON THE EMOTIONAL ROLLERCOASTER OF LIFE

If you were a robot, I could upload any self-help programme and quick as a flash – you'd be upgraded. The new you instantly here! Instead, we have these inconvenient things called feelings that dance around bringing irrational inconsistency to our days. Thankfully however, it's possible to grow an appreciation for ALL the emotions we experience AND to experience a positive state of mind most of the time.

In the words of prolific author Dan Millman: 'You don't have to control your thoughts; you just have to stop letting them control you.'

By the end of this book you'll have a deep understanding of what's driving your emotional rollercoaster and a set of strategies to harness their power and diminish their negative effects.

We'll address fears, develop your capacity to quieten limiting beliefs, and begin to say hello to the voice that says, 'I can handle anything.' The journey to success isn't a straight line, you will have setbacks. By combining grit with a growth mindset we'll reframe failure as the source of unparalleled growth.

And we'll smile too. The rollercoaster has ups and downs,

yes, you will learn how to cope with the downs, but we'll also spend time on the ups. Life is occasionally incredible. Together we'll work out how to increase the frequency and the depth of your happiness.

I truly hope that you enjoy the journey, and I'm here if at any point you'd like to chat about your progress, or your struggles. Drop me an email: todd@ownlife.me.

HOW TO OWN LIFE

This may not be your first book from the Own Life Collection so you'll recognise this guidance, and if you're new to the series, then welcome! ;-).

To truly Own Life takes some time, so be patient with the book and yourself. Give the concepts space to breathe, and your experiments the necessary time to achieve their desired results. In every book in the collection, you'll be learning how to live with greater self-confidence and how to set your path to own your future.

Unlike many self-help books, we are not attempting to turn you into someone new, to add another mask, which is exhausting to live up to. You will always be you, and we want you to be ALL of you, ALL of the time.

When you allow yourself, being you is so easy, and nobody else does it better!

This is your life journey, and this is your book. At the moment the book in your hand looks like anybody else's, but shortly you'll start to add your own notes, in your own way, with your unique handwriting, and instantly this book is like no other on the planet.

Your life too is in your hands. How much you own it depends on how much you invest in it. In a moment you'll be answering a set of questions which will put you on the path to becoming more self-aware, and it's through the lens of 'yourself' that we'll do great work together. Yes, there are models and theories, lots of them in fact, but it's how you relate to them that matters – so when there's a pause in the text and a question for you to ponder, really do it.

Throughout the book, you'll see sections titled 'Reflect & Write'. This is your invitation to do just that. Take some quiet time to consider each of the questions, allow your thoughts and feelings to emerge, and then crystalize them by putting pen to paper. The act of writing down your thoughts helps them to settle in your mind and brings a comforting level of clarity. I don't think of you as readers, I think of you as participants, so read this book with a pen in your hand.

The insights you gain about yourself can be revelatory yet remain merely interesting. To shift the dial of your life requires action, and throughout the book you'll be invited to conduct small experiments to tweak your ingrained behaviours.

From time to time you may have a question that you need some help with; or maybe you'd like to connect with others who are struggling with similar issues; or would like to share a moment of enlightenment, or a piece of advice; or be inspired by other people's Own Life journey. For any of this, head to www.ownlife.me/connect and we'll take this journey together.

HOW'S IT ALL GOING?

Before we start, it's helpful to get a baseline on how things are really going for you. We're starting with a wide lens to check-in on how fully you are Owning Life as a whole. We do this to put *OWNING LIFE WITH COURAGE* into context and to notice which other facets of life you might be able to draw strengths from, or which need additional support so they don't trip you up.

Put a date on the page, and if you've completed this task in previous books in the Own Life collection, do this again first before reading your notes from last time.

Reflect & Write: You've lived on this planet for quite some time now. How's it going? How is life turning out for you? On this occasion you'll notice that I give you a relatively small box to write in. We just want to get an overall impression at this stage.

Perhaps you're thinking, 'It's a huge freakin' mess, and I don't know how to dig myself out.' Or maybe, 'Things are actually going pretty well, but is this it?' No matter how you respond to this question, if you want to get the most out of life, then this book will help you discover the authentic human you are and lay the foundations for living the life you are truly capable of living.

Consider the statements below with real honesty based on your experience of the last six months. Decide to what extent you agree or disagree with each of them, and colour in the corresponding box in the chart on the next page.

1. I know and accept myself for who I am
2. I believe I can become good at anything I choose to put my mind to
3. I maintain a positive emotional state of mind regardless of what is going on around me
4. I push through fear to accomplish things that are uncomfortable
5. What I do is aligned to a deeply held sense of purpose
6. I make the most of life by using my time wisely
7. I am like a battery, always full of energy and ready to go
8. I enjoy trusting, respectful relationships with everyone in my life

	STRONGLY DISAGREE	DISAGREE	NEUTRAL	AGREE	STRONGLY AGREE
1.	☐	☐	☐	☐	☐
2.	☐	☐	☐	☐	☐
3.	☐	☐	☐	☐	☐
4.	☐	☐	☐	☐	☐
5.	☐	☐	☐	☐	☐
6.	☐	☐	☐	☐	☐
7.	☐	☐	☐	☐	☐
8.	☐	☐	☐	☐	☐

Even though it's good to know your start point, there's no need to judge it. Just imagine if you could nudge your scores further to the right? And just imagine what life would be like if you could live it way over to the right-hand column most of the time. That's our goal together.

Wherever you'd like to develop, there's a book in the Own Life collection for you. By fully participating in this book (*OWN LIFE WITH COURAGE*) you will be learning how to manage your emotions and push through fear.

In the future, if you'd like to work on accepting yourself for who you are or becoming the person you want to be, grab the book titled *OWN LIFE WITH CONFIDENCE*. If you want to foster great relationships then *OWN LIFE WITH TRUST* is the book for you. And if you would like to engineer a lifestyle that fulfils your dreams, then *OWN LIFE WITH PURPOSE* is the next book to add to your collection.

Now you have your baseline, are you ready to live a more rewarding life? Sure you are. Let's jump into OWNING LIFE WITH COURAGE.

PART 1

MANAGING 'STATE'

CHAPTER 1
EMOTIONS

Appreciation for Our Human-ness

Have you seen the Disney film *Inside Out*? In it 11-year- old Riley's idyllic life comes crashing down around her when her family moves from Minnesota to San Francisco. The majority of the film is shot inside her head – following characters (the five main emotions) which are controlling her moods and actions: Joy, Sadness, Anger, Disgust, and Fear. Initially, all the characters want Joy to be in control – but the reality is that at various moments, other characters step up to run things. Sadness enables Riley to connect with empathy to her old imaginary friend (Bing Bong), Fear keeps her alive, Anger gets her motivated, and Disgust is the signal that something is deeply offensive or distasteful.

Every one of us has a range of emotions that arise within us, and no-one lives a life of pure joy. Yet many of us have this quest in life to 'simply be happy' – it's a holy grail, and paradoxically, it's the quest that gets in the way of Owning Life. By accepting that 'negative' emotions exist and building an appreciation for psychological discomfort, we can develop 'distress tolerance' – and this is a leading predictor of life success.

Borrowing from the book *The Upside of your Darkside*,[1]

'People who use the full range of their natural psychological gifts are the most healthy, and often, the most successful... The most unwanted negative experiences end up shaping some of the most memorable events of our lives.'

Anger does not have to turn to rage and violence. It can bubble up when we perceive an encroachment on our rights and stir us to defend ourselves and others and maintain boundaries.

Embarrassment is an early warning sign of humiliation; a signal that we've made a small mistake and that a small correction is required. Guilt is a signal that we're violating our moral code and therefore need to adjust our actions (or our code).

To experience a range of emotions is human, and natural, and important. You may wish for endless days of sunshine, but nature knows better; it's only because of the bad-weather-days that we have an environment to enjoy when the clouds clear. So instead of attempting to deny 'negative' emotions and wishing for constant joy, how can you celebrate the colourful lessons the full repertoire brings?

Gratitude for Emotions

Below is a list of emotions, see if you can recall a specific moment in your life when you have felt each one.

Hurt, Angry, Selfish, Hateful, Critical, Sceptical, Jealous, Frustrated, Distant, Confused, Rejected, Helpless, Insecure, Anxious, Inadequate, Discouraged, Embarrassed, Overwhelmed, Guilt, Ashamed, Depressed, Lonely, Bored, Tired, Remorseful, Stupid, Inferior, Isolated, Content, Relaxed, Thoughtful, Intimate, Loving, Trusting, Thankful, Serene, Faithful, Confident, Important, Appreciated, Respected, Worthwhile, Proud, Successful, Surprised,

Hopeful, Optimistic, Cheerful, Creative, Energetic, Excited, Fascinated, Daring, Nurturing, Playful, Joyful.

I encourage you to pause on each word and find some stillness to allow your memory to bring specific moments back to the surface. Place a tick next to each word as you recall a moment in time when you have felt it. There are almost 60 words on the list, so allow yourself to sit for almost a full hour with this exercise.

If you did just pause and allow yourself to daydream, then you will have been on a wonderfully rich journey in your mind. As you brought past experiences to mind, you may have also been reliving the past emotions too – and their physical symptoms. As you stroll through the list, if you really stopped to contemplate a specific situation, you are likely to also now feel how you felt back when the moment happened. At moments, did you notice the heart race? A slight blush? A deep sigh? A smile at the corner of your mouth? An involuntary tightening of some muscles?

You see, our minds and bodies are connected, and this can work either for or against us. We'll explore how, later in this book.

Reflect & Write: If I gave you the option to cross out 50 per cent of the list of emotions and live without ever experiencing those emotions again, would you? What could the long-term negative consequences be of never feeling them again?

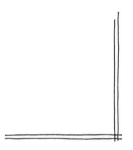

Did you just choose to cross out all the 'negative' emotions? Probably not. You might have been tempted to because of the suffering they have caused you in the past. Yet something stopped you from removing their ability to cause you to suffer in the future. What's most interesting is that on the surface people say they just want to feel happy, AND they want the potential to feel the whole range of emotions over the rest of their life.

E-motion

Originally from the Latin word *emovere* (to move), it wasn't until the early 19th century that the word 'emotion' became attached to feelings, and now we can consider that emotion is 'energy in motion'.

When you recall any one of the above emotions – the moment you felt it most strongly, you were also feeling pretty alive (perhaps except for boredom). Even with serenity, while there's unlikely to be a great deal of visible high energy, there is an internal intensity to it.

Try it now. Select one of the words – choose a positive

emotion (because it's just more fun!). Really bring to mind the last time that you felt it deeply. Close your eyes, count the next three breaths, and then transport yourself back in time. Pay attention to what you notice, tuning into all of your senses of sight, sound, smell, taste and touch. Allow the emotion to rise up, completely immersing your entire body in its light. Then just sit with it and enjoy reliving this positive moment.

Whenever you feel ready, bring yourself back to this moment, and tune into the bodily sensations associated with this emotion. Precisely where in your body do you feel it? Allow this spot to hold your full attention. Mark this spot on the illustration of the body on the previous page and leave your pen resting there.

Notice how the sensation changes and another part of your body calls for attention – allow your awareness to be moved by the changing sensations in your body, and allow your pen to drift across the page to this new spot. Return to the memory with all your attention and notice how the sensation shifts in your body. Keep allowing the pen to drift across the page to represent your internal experience. Stay with this exercise for as long as the body sensation keeps moving.

Take a look at the page. Did you notice that the emotion was dancing around? The energy is in motion, right? It never stays the same, it never stays still. It peaks and it troughs, it tingles, it aches, it is intense, it is teasingly faint. It is all those things, and it will never be exactly the same again.

You've been focussed on a short period when a single emotion was present. If you zoom out and consider a week – perhaps the last week, how many different emotions did you experience? Maybe not many in an I'll-remember-that-moment-for-the-rest-of-my-life way – but I'll bet that if

you are really tuned into the ebb and flow of what's going on inside, you'll experience 50 per cent of the emotions listed every week. Emotions come and go, like clouds. It may look bleak and overcast, as though there is no end to the greyness, and yet you realize some time later that the clouds have thinned, or parted, or completely disappeared.

The challenge we face is that when we see blue skies and try to hold onto a positive emotion like joy, we immediately begin to imagine the loss of this 'positive' emotion and therefore wake ourselves up from the pleasurable experience.

On the other hand, when the skies are grey, we might imagine that there is no end in sight. It's often the worry that things will remain grey that causes us more suffering than the actual emotion itself. So, remember, behind the clouds is a blue sky and it will always emerge. Emotion is energy in motion – so simply give it the freedom to move.

Changing the Climate

Having acknowledged that a great range of emotions come and go, you may also have a prevailing climate – a tendency for the arid conditions of the Sahara, or tropical rains in the equatorial heat, or the six months of darkness followed by six months of light at the Poles. Just as it is possible to take a holiday to a different part of the world, it is also possible to take emotional vacations and even completely change your emotional climate for good. We're just about to learn how.

CHAPTER 2
WHO IS IN THE DRIVING SEAT?

How Many of You Are There?

Set a timer for four minutes. Simply sit with your eyes closed in a quiet space. Feel your breath rise and fall. When you notice a thought arise in your mind, count it and return to your breath and wait. When you notice another thought, count two. And so on.

Pause. Take a break from reading. Close the book. We'll explore your experience in four minutes' time.

How many thoughts arose in your mind? Did you become attached to any of them, whisked away on a journey that you hadn't intended? Did you choose to have those thoughts? If not, who did? And if you were the person having the thought, who was doing the counting?

We have 100,000 thoughts per day, 95 per cent of which can be classified as negative or limiting. You see, you're completely normal, just like everyone else. We are wired this way, and it's one of the many reasons homo sapiens are top dogs.

Emotional Reactions

Our emotions are constantly flowing. This started when we were babies. We were bathed in love, and it felt good. We were shouted at, and it felt bad. Before we had any words to describe our feelings, we were connecting an external stimulus to an internal feeling. And this happens over and over and over again. It becomes autopilot, sometimes we don't know why we feel the way we feel – we just do. The association between an event and a feeling is hardwired deep in our subconscious.

In one experiment, images flashed on a screen in front of a group of volunteers who had electrodes attached to their palms to monitor changes in sweat (an indicator of stress). The images flashed up quicker and quicker – and all contained positive pictures: people smiling, cute dogs, a chocolate bar. The images changed even more quickly, so much so that the participants could no longer tell what each image was before the next one appeared. Within this set of images was a single shot of a scary hairy spider. It was on screen for micro-seconds, and none of the volunteers could recall seeing it. Yet their sweat response indicates they did.

Who is in the driving seat? Your body can react to seeing something you don't even know you saw!

When you turn over the page, before you see any words, you will see an illustration. And perhaps you will also notice an internal reaction to it, even just subtly. A sea of expectant eyes, a lack of smiles, and thousands more people who you can't even make out in the background. A prepared script, a microphone ready to pick up your faltering voice, spotlights exposing the beads of sweat on your brow. Five paces to almost certain humiliation and the end of any chance of a normal life.

Public speaking, the number-one fear.

Notice any body sensations now? You know that you're not about to give that speech – but perhaps your body is starting to shift into fight or flight mode.

Who is in the driving seat? Your body issues distress signals and you may feel anxious despite knowing there is no real threat.

What is more, as we notice the physical sensations, we attach meaning to them: 'My hands are sweaty, I must be nervous about something. What is there to be nervous about?' So you come up with something that makes sense of the sensation. If we asked the spider volunteers if they felt nervous about something, and if so, what – none would

say a spider, but most would come up with some different justification.

Sometimes a thought arises, and we then feel an emotion about that thought. Sometimes it's the opposite; an emotion arises, and we attach thought to it. These two systems are a result of the evolution of the human brain. Around the brain stem is the limbic system (sometimes referred to as the mammalian brain), which is responsible for generating emotions, and processing emotional memories. At the epicentre of this system is the amygdala, which is the first part of the brain to receive sensory information and is responsible for the automatic actions that ensure survival from external threats. Later in human evolution (and later in childhood brain development), come the frontal lobes that deal with planning, thinking, and regulating the emotional excesses of the limbic system.

This area is activated much more slowly, is much less powerful, and as a result, we all occasionally struggle to keep our emotions from running our lives.

In his wonderful book, *The Chimp Paradox*[2], Professor Steve Peters accepts that no matter how hard we try to manage our inner chimp (our emotional self), it is completely normal to have occasional emotional outbursts, because this is simply the way the brain works. Of course, you should try to reduce the negative consequences of your behaviour, but then forgive yourself, you're not perfect (... yet!).

How effectively we manage the interplay between the limbic (emotions) and frontal (logical) systems largely determines our emotional intelligence (which in turn determines our success). We'll return to EI (emotional intelligence) as we conclude this book.

CHAPTER 3
INTERNAL RATHER THAN EXTERNAL

Mood Diary

To what extent is your mood affected by what's happening in the outside world?

Take an audit of the last half-day, walking through moment-to-moment, and make a 'mood diary' of how you felt and what triggered the feeling. For example:

Time	Event	Mood
06:30	Alarm sounds	Tired yet inspired because I've got an exciting day ahead
06:40	Son wakes up a little earlier than usual	Nervous about how my wife feels at being woken up, some sadness that my morning meditation has been interrupted
06:45	Sound of the toilet flushing	Happy that my son has taken himself to the toilet without disturbing anyone

06:50	Son says, 'Cuddles Daddy.'	Love – I won't see him for a while
07:00	Daughter enters the kitchen not wearing her school uniform	Love and suppressed mild disappointment that she hasn't got dressed
07:30	Wife books a social event with friends which clashes with the weekend I'd been planning to take her away for a surprise present	Disappointment, frustration, annoyance, sadness, then guilt after displaying my annoyance
07:45	Daughter picks up her phone and does her 'times tables' app, beating her high score	Pride, satisfaction, contentedness
08:00	Opening bedroom curtains at the front of the house to blue skies and sunshine	Happiness, gratitude

Reflect & Write: Do your own audit now.

What a journey we go on when we really stop to notice it. Most of the time we'd simply get an overall sense of things, and describe the average, i.e. it was a good, bad, or alright morning.

External events trigger internal emotional reactions, which impact your state – this state affects how you encounter the world, and how you respond to it. The extent to which external events impact your internal state is manageable and varies from person to person.

Who do you know that seems to float above day-to-day events, they seem to have some kind of buffer zone protecting their moods? The most emotionally in-control person I know is...

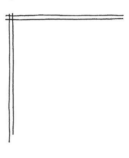

And who is the opposite – their mood is entirely driven by the most recent event or conversation that happened to them? The most emotionally out-of-control person I know is...

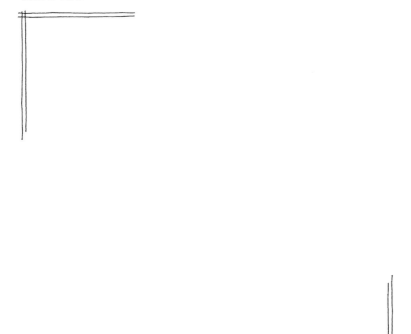

Reflect & Write: If the first person is a 10 (completely able to manage their internal state), and the second person is 0 (their state depends on the external world), what's your number and why do you choose it?

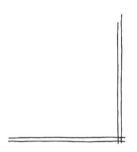

Beliefs Colour External Events

An external event happens, and our emotions are triggered. But how is it that someone next to us, witnessing the same event, seems to feel differently about it?

Take a look at this photograph (credit Phil Noble) Michael Owen (England's third-highest goal scorer and a Liverpool legend), has just missed a golden opportunity to score and win an important match in the dying seconds. Notice the common reaction – Michael's (lying on the floor) hands on his head, and all of his teammates, and every fan behind the goal all mimicking Michael, hands on their heads.

External event (missed shot), internal reaction (disappointment), automatic behaviour (hands on the head, and mouths wide open).

But look a little closer (it's like a Where's Wally challenge), can you spot two fans with raised fists, clearly in celebration. In colour, this photo shows these two fans are wearing yellow, in contrast to the red of the Liverpool fans. For them: external event (missed shot), internal reaction (elation), automatic behaviour (fist raised, shout of triumph). You clearly see two different responses to the same external stimulus.

Why? In this case, it's obvious – they have different beliefs. One person believes that Liverpool is the best team in the world, the other that Manchester United are. Our beliefs and values alter our perception of an external event. As William Shakespeare famously wrote in *Hamlet*: 'Nothing is either good or bad, but thinking makes it so.'

It turns out that our level of happiness has little to

do with the environment in which we live, instead it is related to our interpretation of it. Michael Neill puts it nicely: 'we live in a world of thought, but we think we live in a world of external experiences'. In other words, we often can't tell the difference between the world that we have constructed in our imagination and the real one. The mind projects what it sees onto the canvas of reality rather than acting as a camera to accurately record reality.

This means that we all make up stuff that simply isn't there (sound familiar?)! So remember, just because a thought is in your head, it doesn't mean it's true.

Different Experiences

Consider some recent examples from your life where your response differed from someone else's. There's no need to defend, justify or rationalise the different responses for now, simply acknowledge them.

Here's an example. Earlier this week, my wife, daughter and I walked past a scruffy young man huddled against the cold, clearly homeless, and begging for money. Here are the first words each of us uttered:

Olive (my 10-year-old daughter): 'Mum, can we take him home and give him a shower?'

Tammy (my wife): 'Todd, do you have any money on you?'

Me: 'Society is so broken that it allows victims to sleep on the street.'

On our local Facebook group, the variety of responses increases: 'Why doesn't he get a job, the rest of us have to work?' 'He's the eyes and ears of the drug gangs.' 'He's collecting £150 per day, don't give him your cash.' 'The majority of homeless guys suffer from mental health illness, give the guy a break.' 'More than half the people begging on the streets of our town are not genuinely homeless'.

'Spare change or real change. Give your money to the homeless charity who make sure it gets well used for the right things.'

You see, we all walked along the same street and saw the same guy. But our emotional responses ranged from pity to anger, from contempt to sorrow.

Reflect & Write: Your turn. What recent sight, event, show, news headline, etc. caused you to have a different reaction to some people around you?

The 'World' is Created in the Mind

It's sometimes quite easy to notice the symptoms of different perspectives, but what is the cause?

Our five senses receive four million bits of information every second, the vast majority of which don't enter our conscious awareness as it's simply impossible for us to process it all. For example, until I mention it, and you read these words, you're probably not aware of the physical sensation of your foot on the floor. But now you are aware. The sensory data was always there – your subconscious had taken the decision that this was unimportant information for you to know and had therefore deleted it.

All the time, you are deleting more than 90 per cent of the available sensory information – and unaware of what you're deleting. It simply isn't in your awareness. The person sitting next to you may have very similar sensory inputs but is deleting different information. Therefore, their experience of the same moment is different from yours. Our filters are based on values, beliefs, memories, personality, and attitude, and they are as unique as your thumbprint. If you're interested in finding out more about the filters that you see the world through check out *Own Life with Confidence*.

These filters determine not only what we delete, but also how our minds distort things – misrepresenting reality and causing us to jump at shadows and 'see' evidence of a homeless man being involved in drug supply.

Finally, we have a 'generalization' filter – a process of learning and drawing conclusions so information can be used again without having to go through a reanalysis every time we come across something similar. For example, phobias often result from a one-time event that has been generalized to be perceived as an every-time event. It is the brain process of generalization that causes us to make instant judgements about new people we meet based on our past experience with similar-looking people.

The end result of all this filtering is that we are not living in the real world, we are subconsciously creating a fantasy world that, to us, accurately represents the outer world. Yet it is distorted. We then have thoughts and emotions about this fantasy world rather than the real one; and these affect our behaviour, which in turn, shapes the world that we experience.

To some, a social occasion is full of opportunities to exchange stories with interesting people. If this is how you perceive an event, interesting conversations are likely to take place. However, for other people the same event is perceived as threatening, and perhaps an opportunity to be ignored by people who believe themselves to be more interesting. Hence this is what happens.

Sometimes known as the 'law of attraction', you get more of what you spend time thinking about, because without knowing it, you are creating it! So, to dial-up or down any emotion, you can choose to work on influencing your external environment or on your internal interpretation of the external world.

And it's the second option that allows you to Own Life. You can change your filters, and this is what we'll look at next.

CHAPTER 4

PROGRAMMING THE MIND

Gratitude Habit

In a moment I want you to try something I learnt from inspiring public speaker Steve Head. Look at the sums below, take a few seconds to digest them – and then say a single word out loud. Ready? Go.

1x1 = 1
2x2 = 4
3x3 = 9
4x4 = 15

Did you say 'wrong'?

In fact, 75 per cent of the sums are right, yet we're programmed to notice what's wrong. When there are no tea bags left in the cupboard, we moan, and it can set up a day of noticing everything wrong. The traffic, the weather, the temperature in the office, the pen clicking of the person next to us. Yet we rarely notice the 100 previous days when there was a tea bag in the cupboard.

Reflect & Write: A common filter that we carry is to notice the 15s (the things that go wrong in life), rather than the 1, 4, 9s (the good stuff). So, rebalance this for today by writing a long list of all the little things that have already gone well.

Reflect & Write: Continuing from the last exercise, consider anything and everything that you are grateful for and write a list of at least 10 things (and keep on going if they keep on coming!).

How do you feel now? Probably, really good. This good feeling can have a lasting effect, and change your behaviour, which impacts your results, which makes you feel good. It's a positive cycle that starts with gratitude, and it's a wonderful habit to foster.

Every day, at the same time, take a pen and paper and write down three things that you are grateful for. Attempt never to repeat anything you've written before. Do this for 21 straight days and notice how you feel.

At the start of the practice, everything you write might feel like THE BIG STUFF: my family; a roof over my head; peace in my neighbourhood; food in the cupboard. But as you challenge yourself to come up with novel things to write, you begin to appreciate the small stuff too. The buds appearing on the cherry tree; the dawn arriving minutes

earlier each spring day; the feeling of calm when shaking off the work shoes in the evening; the little bird that hopped across your path and gave a merry tweet!

You may like to do this using pen and paper. I like to use an app, and it's about time I mentioned my favourite app of all time. It's the app I've recommended to more than 2,000 people and I believe that if you create the habit of sticking to it every day, then you're guaranteed to increase how much you Own Life. It's called the 'Five Minute Journal', by Intelligent Change Inc. Check it out on your phone right now. It will change your life.

In the morning, the five-minute journal first asks you to record three things you're grateful for. It then asks, 'what will I do to make today great?' There's then a single line for you to write a daily affirmation. This is something that you are good at – it's turning 1,4,9 on yourself.

In the evening, there's a moment to reflect and record 'three amazing things that happened today'. This makes you replay the day in your mind, asking your brain to go searching for the highlights – and it's amazing how many there are when you really go looking. After a while, you'll begin to register these amazing things as they happen, thinking to yourself 'I might write that tonight.'

There's also space to record one photo. I now have a collection of hundreds of images – recording a highlight of every day of my last few years. It's such a joy to occasionally flick through them – an instant state shifter and smile generator. If you don't fancy the app, do what my daughter did, and fill a notebook.

To make sure you've got no reason not to start doing this today, I've included your first 30 days of journal pages at the back of this book. It's such a powerful habit to get into, I suggest you don't wait until you reach the end of the book before commencing it. Get started right now. Turn to Part 3: Daily Journal, put today's date on the first page and complete the top half of the page. Before you go to bed, complete the bottom half. Then keep this rhythm going for the next 30 days. You literally have everything you need in your hands right now.

The Computer

We learnt earlier how the limbic system (emotional brain) reacts quicker than the frontal system (rational brain) – and how we can be in the grips of emotion and reacting to it without feeling there is space between external stimulus and internal response. It's then very hard for your relatively weak rational brain to regain control.

The better strategy is to develop the antidote so that the emotional response doesn't activate in the first place. Steve Peters refers to the parietal lobe of the brain as the computer, with two functions: to think and act automatically for you using programmed thoughts and behaviours; and as a reference source for information, beliefs and values. The parietal system (computer), works faster than either the limbic (emotional) or the frontal (rational) systems and therefore outperforms them both.

By programming the computer with useful autopilots, we can eliminate some negative emotion-driven behaviours. For example, when I'm driving and make way for someone to pass down a narrow street, and they don't bother to raise a hand in thanks, my immediate emotional response used to be anger (which could stay with me for a while and affect my driving).

With the space to think and the benefit of hindsight, my rational brain has (over the years) caught up with this negative consequence to an external stimulus and programmed the computer not to respond negatively. Now, when the same situation occurs, my instant computer response is of calm, and my emotional response is joy, my behaviour is to smile as I remember that I am capable of managing my inner chimp.

The Body-Mind Connection

Do you remember how when you recalled past positive experiences you felt an actual sensation in your body, and your posture may well have changed as a result? It works the other way around too. If you hold a slouchy, low energy posture, you will feel lethargic, unenthusiastic, and bored. If you walk tall, stand upright, sit with a straight back – then you will feel more awake, more energized, more ready for life. The mind and body are connected, so let's see how we can use the body to affect our state.

Recall something that you are wonderfully proud of.

Pause.

Really remember it.

Now notice how the feeling of pride washes around your body, paying attention to any sensation in any particular part. Allow your posture to change so that the feeling of pride swells. Notice your breath rising and falling, and the sensation of your heart beating.

Insert some words into your feelings and say to yourself 'I feel strong.' And believe that you are. Adjust your posture, so you feel physically firmer but without straining. Repeat the words 'I feel strong' and notice how your body naturally reacts to the words.

We've created a congruent loop whereby body and mind are 'saying' the same thing. Capture the body feeling. Capture its shape in your memory, because in the future, by taking this posture, you will be triggering the connected emotions of strength and pride. This body strength will bring mental strength to your future challenges.

Reflect & Write: Give this strong feeling, and strong posture a label. It doesn't matter what it is, and it doesn't have to make sense to anyone else. What word, or couple of words could you say to yourself that would remind you of this feeling?

Strong Morning Habits

Consider the start of your day. The alarm goes off. What happens next? The first thought: 'It's too early, I need some more sleep, I'm comfy here, I've got a bit more time.' And the first action? Hit the snooze button. (I use my iPhone as my alarm, and the snooze button is 10 times the size of the stop button – Apple is willing me to hit snooze!) Then what? The alarm goes off again. A quick mental calculation, 'What's happening first thing today? Can I afford another five minutes in bed?... Yes.' Second action? Hit snooze. Eventually, you can hit snooze no longer. 'Damn, I've really got to get up now.'

You drag yourself from beneath the safe comfort of your duvet and into a cold room, and switch on autopilot – coffee, breakfast, shower, coffee, search for clothes, search for keys, leave the house not a moment sooner than you have to, commute in a daze, arrive and begin the first interaction with colleagues: 'How are you? ... OK.' Coffee.

Would you consider this to be a strong start to your day? Is your posture when arriving at work glowing with strength and pride? What message are you giving to others as they interact with you?

Every day, at some point, if it's going to be a great day, you have to shift from this weak state to a strong one. You've established a poor habit – a deeply ingrained morning routine that requires daily willpower to overcome, and it's time to create a new one.

Even if you've got a voice that says 'I am not a morning person' it doesn't have to be on permanent repeat for the rest of your life. So how about switching to a growth mindset and changing your story right now? 'I'm not a morning person, yet.'

Can you allow yourself to believe that change is possible? You wouldn't be reading this book if you didn't.

Reflect & Write: Rate your typical morning zero (weak) to ten (strong) – where are you currently? And why do you score it this way?

Reflect & Write: Suspending judgement for a moment, if you could achieve a perfect 10, what impact would this have? If I could start every morning wonderfully, then...

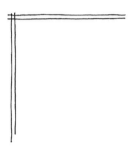

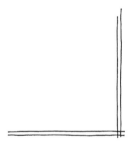

Now create a plan for your strong morning start. Some things others have done that may inspire you are: leave the phone in a different room, select a good track to wake up to, change your alarm sound, choose the clothes for tomorrow before bedtime, buy and prepare breakfast the night before, use the Five Minute Journal app, wake 15 minutes earlier and do something you enjoy, write down your good intention for the day, go to bed earlier and don't watch your phone in bed, buy a new lovely smelling shampoo.

Reflect & Write: Get creative, how could you get closer to a perfect 10? What new morning routine would you like to foster?

Now, remember, just because you just wrote it down doesn't mean it's automatically going to happen. If only life was that simple! No, it's going to take deep reserves of willpower, and you don't possess endless supplies of willpower. So let's put in place some willpower strategies from the *Own Life with Confidence* book. Your chimp brain wakes up way faster than your rational brain and it will sabotage your good intentions before you've even had chance to notice.

Looking at your list above, what preparations can you make so that it's as simple as possible to do the things you want to, and super-hard to re-run your customary morning routines? Let's take an example. The snooze button is the Achilles' heel of many people, but they stick with the default iPhone alarm clock with its giant button of temptation. Instead of relying on the willpower of the rational brain within the first 5 seconds of being awake, let's remove the temptation. I just googled 'alarm clock apps without a snooze button', and found this cool article titled '8 Apps Guaranteed to Wake You Up'.

The first app on the list is called the Walk Up Alarm Clock with the strapline 'imagine an alarm that blares at you until you get out of bed and literally walk around'. OK, it will get me out of bed but I'm pretty sure it would put me in a foul mood. It's not the app for me – maybe it's the one that you need? I'll keep looking for the right one for me. What I'm not going to do is have the same external stimulus and expect myself to be able to come up with a different response first thing in the morning.

Reflect & Write: What will you do that gives you the best possible chance of making at least one of the strong morning intentions to stick?

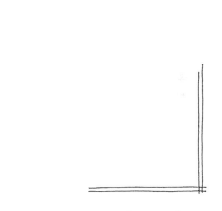

Set a target to keep doing the new routine for 21 days, because if you do, then this strong routine becomes your new habit and it will take more effort to break it than to stick to it. Ready to start the day well? If you do, then everything that comes afterwards will flow more easily. Go on. You can do it.

A Wake-up Call

Our negative morning mindset can begin very young – conditioned into us by parents. My daughter was always a good sleeper, and when she woke in the mornings, we'd hear her singing to herself in bed with quiet contentment. For several years, I was able to begin my morning on my terms, with a strong routine.

Until Wilbur, my son, arrived on a frosty January morning in 2014.

He was the opposite. He wakes early, and for him, being awake meant that everyone else should be too – he was ready to start his day. The deal with my wife was that, before 5 a.m., she'd get up and settle him again. After 5 a.m., it was my job to quietly start the day. Only I wasn't ready to start my day!

I'd hear him, check the clock, (curse that it was 5:05 a.m. and therefore my job), wander slowly to his room rubbing my eyes while knowing that if I didn't walk quickly, the whole house would be awake. As I entered my son's room he'd be standing up in his cot, 'Daddy, Daddy, Daddy,' he'd cheerfully chant.

'Son, why are you awake so early? Why can't you go back to sleep? Come on, give Dad a break!'

It was this way for many, many months. Then I realized something. I was teaching people about the importance of beginning the day right, and yet every day my son was naturally starting his day strong – full of energy, full of inspiration, full of love, and joy, and smiles. The first thing he experienced was his dad telling him that he wasn't wanted right now, that he was somehow wrong to be ready for another amazing day on planet Earth.

He only had a vocabulary of a few words, and yet already he was learning that mornings should be rejected. Deep in his brain, I was responsible for joining up synapses that would be with him for life. It was a wake-up call – what brain connections would I like him to have?

I embarked on a programme of resetting my own morning habits – retraining my brain to have different thoughts – setting up my computer auto-response that is faster than my chimp. How could I enable my son to have a 10/10 morning? It takes time, and lots of false starts, but I can tell you that it is possible.

Now when I hear my son in the morning I am overcome with gratefulness – I have trained my brain to have an automatic first thought, 'I have a son, and he loves me, I am truly blessed.'

Strong Daily Habits

Now you've considered your morning routine, how about the rest of the day. What positive habits would you like to establish that keep you strong? Would any of the following be helpful?

- When asking someone 'How are you?' pause, and wait for a response rather than continuing with your task.

- Create energising breaks to your work – plan to focus for 50 minutes and do something recharging for 10 minutes.
- Get outside at least once – perhaps a brisk walk at lunchtime.
- Consider your nourishment – eat healthy snacks throughout the day.
- Replace coffee with something else.
- Notice your posture at work. If you're slouched, then your output will be slouched. Would a different seat work better for you?
- Is your workplace tidy, and free from distraction?
- How can you make the most of your commute? Listen to a podcast on an interesting topic?

If it feels too much of a stretch to be like this all day take a tip from Elbert Hubbard: 'Be pleasant until ten o'clock in the morning and the rest of the day will take care of itself.'

Reflect & Write: Once you've started your day right, how would you like to continue it? Complete this sentence: My days will be strong because I'm going to...

CHAPTER 5
EXPECTATIONS

The Happiness Equation

Mo Gawdat was a Google executive, successful in the trappings of life, but deeply unhappy. His quest for happiness led him to a simple equation:

Happiness = reality – expectation

He was severely tested when he lost his son to a routine operation at the age of 21. When he talks about losing his son, Mo explains that nothing he could do, and no amount of crying could bring him back. He had to reset things. Make today, day zero. Then work each day to make it slightly better. We often wish the world was a certain way, no poverty, for example, or friendly smiles from colleagues – but when these wishes become unrealistic expectations, then we find the source of unhappiness.

What I take from Mo's advice is to have acceptance that the world is imperfect, unfair, and sometimes harsh. Therefore, when I come across an example of this, I'm not crushed by its emotional impact, but simply inspired by the belief that I have the potential to make the reality just slightly better. And the first day of this process can start when I'm at rock bottom. Day zero could be today.

Allowing Things to Simply 'Be'

What can you control?

Your own response to the external world, and nothing else. You may have some influence over what happens in your environment, or how other people behave, but you certainly can't control them.

Suffering happens, and if you have built an over-optimistic fantasy that it won't, you will live an 'if only' life. One in which the true events don't match your idealized imaginary ones. Should you lower your expectations? Imagine that tomorrow will really be terrible, and then be happy when things are not as bad as you'd imagined? That doesn't feel like a recipe for happiness either. So, what's the answer?

Have hopes, have dreams, be inspired by how great tomorrow can be. Have expectations of how you will respond to external events but let go of any fantasy that tomorrow will match the world you've imagined. When a moment arises, allow it to be exactly as it is – without judgement, and take pride in your ability to maintain your state regardless of external stimulus.

Reflect & Write: When you are considering the next 48 hours, what expectations do you have? What range of possible scenarios exist – from the very worst to the very best? How could you respond to the extremes?

Now let go of expecting it to be wonderful or awful; chances are that it will fall between the two. But regardless of what transpires, you now know that your inner world doesn't have to reflect it.

It's in Your Mind

I recently watched a talk by Gen Kelsang Nyema (a Buddhist nun) where she started by asking the audience three questions:

1. Are you having a good day?
2. Why? (what's behind your previous response?)
3. Tomorrow, would you rather have a good day or a bad day?

How would you respond to these questions? If you're like me, the answer to the final question is, of course, 'I want a good day'. But when you look at your response to the second question, what is it that you have listed as your reasons for today being good or bad? It's a list of things that happened, right! Circumstances you largely can't control. Therefore, you may wish for tomorrow to be good, but the reality is it's out of your control, leading to yo-yoing happiness.

We need to stop outsourcing our happiness to other people and events and blaming them for our unhappiness. We need to start cultivating a source of happiness that comes from the inside. We need to start Owning Life.

Happiness and unhappiness are states of mind, and therefore their real causes can't be found outside the mind. It isn't what is happening, it's how we respond to what's happening that determines happiness, and this comes from our state of mind.

How do we cultivate a reliable, peaceful state of mind? Right now, sit comfortably with your feet gently resting on the floor and notice the movement of your breath through your nostrils, and soften your gaze so the world becomes blurred while just about being able to read these words.

Breathe out agitation, any busyness or frustration as if it was dark smoke. Breathe in clear, bright light, the nature of inner peace, imagining it filling your entire body and mind.

As you continue to notice the sensation of your breathing, imagine the dark smoke leaving every pore in your body and being replaced by clear, bright light.

Now just sit and enjoy the inner peace that arises. Be patient. Give yourself some time right now to just pause. When you are ready to move on, feel determined to bring this inner peace into the rest of your day.

Meditation is the mental action of concentrating on a peaceful, positive state of mind and can be as simple as the few minutes you have just experienced. Load this simple technique into your brain's parietal (computer) system by fostering it as a daily practice, and then notice how easy it is to have a good day, every day.

At any moment in time, we can pause, turn our attention inwards and enquire about our current state of mind. We can't always rationalize why it is the way it is, or why we feel different from other people who seem to be in similar situations. Your emotions will ebb and flow every moment of life, and you really wouldn't choose it any other way. You can experience an inner smile more often by cultivating positive morning routines and daily gratitude. Next, we'll tackle some of the more difficult emotions, but before launching into all that, allow the edges of your mouth to turn up a little – give yourself an inner grin.

PART 2

FEAR, FAILURE AND GRIT

CHAPTER 6
WHAT ARE YOU AFRAID OF?

Fear can prevent you from living the life of your dreams. I know this is true for you because it's true for everyone. So feel OK about this, you are completely normal.

In her famous book *Feel the Fear and Do It Anyway*, Susan Jeffers explains that in most cases the inability to deal with fear is not a psychological problem; it is one that the mind can be educated to overcome. In Part 2, you will learn how to push through resistance and begin to take control of the future.

Fear Spotting

Have you ever been in a classroom with a tutor, or perhaps a meeting with a boss and a fair few other people and the discussion is energized and interesting, and fast flowing. As the debate develops, you get a thought. A good thought. It may be a question, a comment, a challenge, a reference. It's something that could really change the direction of the conversation. It really is a very, very good thought. While the conversation continues around you, you begin to get excited, you feel it in your stomach. You begin to rehearse in your mind what you will say, and what other brilliant ideas you can link to it. Your thoughts continue as you begin to re-engage with what's happening in the room. Space arises, no one is talking, and it's the perfect moment for you to insert your idea. You know this is the moment.

And you do nothing.

You let the moment pass. You haven't contributed your potential, and the discussion is weaker for it. Luckily, someone else in the room makes the exact same point. And everyone else pats them on the back, 'What a great comment!' they all say. And inwardly you're thinking, 'That was my point.' Outwardly you may say, 'I was going to say that!' The question is, what stopped you from stepping forward?

Fear. It wasn't there when you had the initial thought but grew from a tiny seed into a rampant tree within your own mind, although nothing had changed in the external environment. But fear of what? In this case, something called sociophobia (the fear of making a fool of yourself in front of other people – 'is my thought actually silly?'). It's the most common phobia. Included within its sphere are public speaking, talking to strangers, networking and new groups of people.

Reflect & Write: You too may occasionally suffer from sociophobia and can recognize the anxiousness it generates. What other things cause you to feel anxious? Let's collect all of them now, how long a list can you generate?

Reflect & Write: In the sociophobia example above, the fear of being judged causes people not to speak up. What are you not doing because you feel anxious?

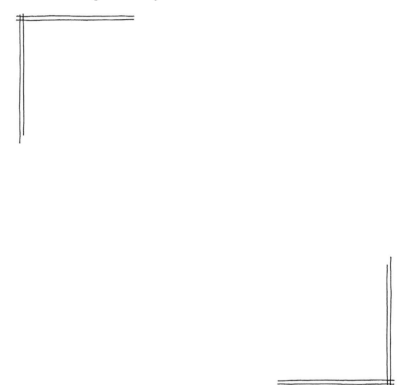

You see, your fears are holding you back. If you allow yourself to dream of a wonderful future, of achieving all of your potential, and being wonderfully successful, then the butterflies automatically start. You will never eradicate fear for as long as you are exposed to something new and different (which is almost daily!). So we can all stop trying to remove fear from our lives – IT IS NOT GOING TO HAPPEN. Through this chapter, you will learn to understand the nature of fear, and how to release yourself from its powerfully limiting grip.

Everyone Is Afraid

It may be reassuring to know that some of the fears you just wrote about are very common. Did you have any of these themes coming up? Tick any that apply to you:

1. I don't like to try radically new things (fear of uncertainty).
2. I'm not really good enough, and I will be found out (fear of inadequacy).
3. I wish things could stay the way they are (fear of change).
4. My life is passing me by (fear of missing out).
5. If I try, I may not succeed (fear of failure).
6. I may look stupid (fear of being judged).
7. People may not like me (fear of rejection).

If you could take a look at 100 notebooks, you'd find that the majority of the above statements are ticked for the majority of people. Why is this the case? Surely the human species could have evolved to eliminate these limiting thoughts? Keep reading, and soon you will be thankful that the opposite is true.

Homo Sapiens

Like all animals, human beings have evolved ways to help protect ourselves from danger. Our senses constantly scan for signs of danger, and these inputs are sent directly to the amygdala (the almond-shaped set of neurons existing in all vertebrates), which tells the body to respond automatically, and instantly (before the rational human brain catches up).

Two systems are activated: the sympathetic nervous system uses nerve pathways to initiate responses in the body, and the adrenal-cortex system uses the bloodstream.

The combined effect of these two systems is the fight-or-flight response, causing changes in the body that include:

- Heart rate and blood pressure increase.
- Pupils dilate to take in as much light as possible.
- Veins in the skin constrict to send more blood to the major muscle groups (sometimes described as 'chilling' as a result of the hands and feet feeling cold).
- Blood-glucose level increases.
- Some muscles tense as they are energized by adrenaline and glucose (responsible for goosebumps).
- Other muscles relax to allow more oxygen into the lungs (which can also affect bladder control).
- Nonessential systems (like digestion) shut down to allow more energy to be directed to the emergency functions.
- Trouble focussing on small tasks (the brain is directed to focus only on the big threats).

When faced with a physical threat, these automatic responses help us to survive. For the 200,000 years of homo sapiens' evolution, it is this feature of our brains that kept our ancestors alive and is the reason we exist today. I am grateful that the automatic fear response has survived the process of human evolution!

Modern-day Emotional Threats
When your ancestors began to migrate from the African plains, they faced daily physical threats, and you too may occasionally face real physical dangers – in which case these body responses are helpful.

We also frequently face psychological threats. Remember the illustration of the lectern and the masses of expectant faces. Imagine it now. The audience is settling down in their seats. They include your colleagues, your boss, and all the important people in your academic field, your friends and family, and a considerable number of the public who have paid to hear you talk. The microphone has been tested, the audience goes quiet, and the compere introduces you. Five paces away, up a handful of steps is the podium, and a sea of eyes all turned in your direction. The chatter in the room subsides to leave a hush of anticipation; the next voice to be heard by the entire congregation will be yours.

Reflect & Write: As you imagine this scenario, notice how you are feeling. Write down the sensations that you are noticing in your body right now.

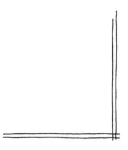

Do you actually feel those sensations as you sit here reading this sentence? They aren't imagined. The feelings are real, right here, right now – even though the scenario is made up. You are not actually going to give that presentation, your rational brain knows this, but your amygdala has reacted and set into motion all the symptoms of fight-or-flight. The body responds to emotional threats, be they real or not, and you can't prevent it from happening.

Our goal is therefore to accept the facts of evolution and instead create strategies the rational brain can use to either reduce the negative impact of the body's stress response or cause it to be activated less frequently. Where there is no physical threat, our goal is to reduce the distracting noise caused by the body so that the rational brain can simply get on with performing its job.

CHAPTER 7
PUSHING
THROUGH FEAR

I Just Can't Handle It

Look at the list of fears you made earlier. If we added your list to mine, and to my daughter's, and to that of everyone else reading this book, we'd end up with a very long list of things to fear. These things are likely to have external triggers, but the feeling of fear comes from within.

Jeffers introduces the idea of 'level 2' fears which have to do with the inner states of mind: 'They are not situation-oriented, they involve the ego' and include rejection, success, failure, being conned, helplessness, disapproval and loss of image.

Level 2 fears are simply thoughts about external events, so what's causing them to turn into the physical symptoms of fear?

Regardless of which of the thousands of external fear-inducing situations you could be faced with, they all come to the same apex and the feeling that 'I just can't handle it'.

To eliminate the effect of fear on your life, you don't have to control the outside world, you simply have to develop the capacity to manage your internal state, and then trust that you have that capacity whenever it is called upon. By having solid self-belief, you have the answer to managing fear. What can we get started with now to diminish the impact of fear?

Wouldn't it be cool to know that when you come across things you fear, you could sit serenely with a confident inner voice that says, 'I can handle it,' allowing your intelligent brain to focus on simply being your natural self?

It's Not as Bad as I Thought It Would Be
Fear of something will persist until you do it and reflect on it. When facing a fear, your options are:

1. Remain afraid of it forever, or
2. Step into the fear and just do it.

'@$?&!!! Where's the nice option?'

Have you ever said to yourself, 'That wasn't as bad as I thought it would be'? Of course you have. This is because your mind was having a wonderful time fantasising for hours (sometimes days, weeks, months, and years) about just how bad a catastrophe could unfold if you dared to step into the situation. The reality is never quite so bad.

Reflect & Write: What things have turned out not to be quite as bad as you imagined?

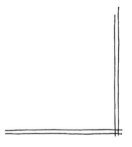

Here's an interesting statistic, over 90 per cent of what we worry about never happens. As Dale Carnegie says, 'Remember, today is the tomorrow you worried about yesterday.'

Reflect & Write: Do you have any examples of things you used to worry about, but no longer do? If so, how did you overcome them?

'Just Do It' Evidence

What's interesting is that the more times we face a fear and push through it, the more confidence we have that we can push through the next one. There's a snowball effect. Those people who shy away from uncomfortable feelings at every turn will find more and more things to feel uncomfortable about, while those that face them head-on, and actually seek them out, find that fewer and fewer everyday things induce a sense of fear.

Reflect & Write: Let's start small. Of the tiny things that you have typically avoided, which do you plan to stop avoiding from today? List five.

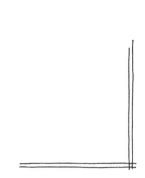

When the circumstance arises, just do them. Then reflect on it afterwards – was it better or worse than you feared? Did you say to yourself, 'That wasn't as bad as I thought?'

Everyday Courage

Each time you tackle something uncomfortable, you draw on your reserves of courage. If you stepped into any one of the above situations, then congratulations, you deserve a pat on the back. It took courage. You may be able to identify people who show unfathomable courage. I'm currently reading *Cold* by Ranulph Fiennes, (a modern-day explorer and the first person to circumnavigate the globe pole to pole), he seems to have bottomless reserves of courage. I don't have what he has, and in comparison to Ranulph perhaps you don't perceive yourself as a courageous person.

But a technique that can help is the '5-Second Rule' conceived by motivational speaker Mel Robbins (check out her TED talk 'How to Stop Screwing Yourself Over'). When I have taken a decision to do something that feels challenging, unless I act on it quickly, my brain finds a thousand reasons not to start. So, I apply the '5-Second Rule'. Now when I hesitate before doing something that I know I should, I count backwards 5-4-3-2-1, and then I do it. In the instant, as I say the word 'zero', I take action.

Robbins says, 'If you don't act on an instinct within that five-second window, that's it. You're not doing it.'

Go back to your list of fears. If overthinking is getting in your way and you're procrastinating, have a go at applying Mel's '5 Second Rule'.

Expanding Your Comfort Zone

The above exercise nudges at the boundaries of your comfort zone, making it marginally bigger, but you probably have some fears that sit well outside it – let's call these 'zone fivers'. All your fears can now be categorized depending on the scale of the anxiety that they induce.

Reflect & Write: Take one of the fears you wrote down – now, right now, imagine doing that thing. Notice how your body reacts to the thought of it, and give it a rating. Then do the same for the rest of your fears.

1. it's in my comfort zone
2. it's on the edge but not really a big thing to overcome
3. it's definitely uncomfortable, and I'm getting some noticeable physical symptoms
4. I can't really be rational about it, my chimp brain is taking over
5. it's so far from happening that it feels unreal and therefore I'm not actually too concerned about it

With the experiments in the last section, you've begun to eat into zone 2. Remember, the fear exists until it is faced. So, what else is in your zone 2 that you're going to face? Once you've tackled these, you'll observe that zone 3 things are no longer out of reach, some of them are simply at the new edge of the comfort zone. From your list above, circle two or three which you feel you'll address next.

Just for fun, imagine that over the next year, you go on a fear-busting crusade and successfully expand your comfort zone all the way to include zone 4. You're on a roll, and next up is one of the big ones in zone 5.

Reflect & Write: Select the most exciting one. If you could face this fear and make it feel comfortable, what difference would it make to your life? If you knew you wouldn't fail, what would you attempt to do?

CHAPTER 8
REFRAMING FEAR

Big Fear, Little Fear

Fear can paralyse, or it can stimulate strong determination. And you get to choose. If I were to fear a life of loneliness, I could take the victim mindset and find all the reasons why this could come true and spiral into a fear of rejection. I might avoid socializing to prevent feeling rejected, and therefore become lonelier. Or I use the fear to give me a kick up the arse. I fear the significant psychological damage caused by loneliness. I am motivated to engage in activities that feel on the edge of my comfort zone to combat it. If the fear of loneliness wasn't there, I might lack the motivation to push through short-term discomfort.

Reflect & Write: What significant long-term fear do you have, and what uncomfortable things do you need to confront in the short-term for you to feel better? What's the worst that could happen if you stepped into the little fear? (Run these questions through for five different big fears.)

Discomfort in Too Much Comfort

When things get too comfortable, they get boring. Time passes, life goes by. You are this amazing unique human being, built to experience life and contribute to society. Sitting in a comfortable harbour actually induces a sense of restlessness that can feel, ironically, uncomfortable. Those feelings that dance within us when we test the edge of our comfort zone help us feel alive. Next time you sense them, be grateful.

You want to find the sweet spot between feeling totally out of control and thrown about by storms, versus lazily watching time float by, stuck in the doldrums. If you want to achieve your potential, you need to happily explore the limits, and then take action to add or remove excitement. Franklin D Roosevelt said it nicely: 'A smooth sea never made a skilled sailor.'

Is It Just Excitement?

Consider something that you would be wonderfully excited about doing. Not just a little bit, I mean super-excited. Next week I go to South Africa with my wife, and I'm so excited about the moment when we've picked up our hired 4x4 camper, got comfortable with how it drives, left the city behind us, and pulled off from a highway onto an empty gravelled country road with the sun low in the sky in the rear-view mirror, mountains in the distance, and vineyards either side.

Wow, I'm already there!

Pick your wonderfully exciting moment. What is it? Visualize it clearly in your mind or write it down if you prefer. Now allow yourself to fully experience this future moment. Imagine all the details, run it like a movie trailer, add the sounds and smells. Keep it running. Gaze gently out of the window as you daydream. Allow your imagination to carry you away.

Reflect & Write: How does it feel to visualize your fantasy moment? What sensations do you notice in your body right now?

Do you notice the similarities between the physical symptoms we connect with the word 'excitement', and the symptoms we connect with the word 'fear'? Almost identical, right? So how about this for an audacious flip of perception: When you feel these same physical symptoms and automatically label them as 'being afraid', instead, consciously give it a new label – 'the excitement of facing something new'.

Yes, I was sceptical at first, too. Then I tried it with public speaking. I'm a professional facilitator of events, and every time before they start my pulse races, my stomach gets queasy, I go to the loo quite a lot, my palms (and armpits) sweat, I compulsively check my notes, my speech gets quicker, and my eyes dart back and forth.

When I label these symptoms as 'nerves', they get worse, and I can believe that I'm going to forget my words or go bright red. But when I started to label my symptoms as 'wide-eyed excitement' and being grateful for the adrenaline that is making me alert, then the rising symptoms become OK. Now, years later, it is with welcome relief that these feelings arise. If they ever don't come, then it's time for me to do something new as I'll be in my comfort zone and no longer bringing my 'A' game to every event.

Cock-ups

Occasionally you put off starting something important because you're worried about messing it up. You procrastinate over decisions because the over-analysis of the chimp brain has convinced you that one path leads to almost certain humiliation, pain and suffering – but you don't know which one. The easy option is to do nothing and let the outside world decide your destiny. But for you to Own Life, you've got to make the decision. In an increasingly

VUCA world (volatile, uncertain, complex, ambiguous), you will have to make decisions that aren't black and white, meaning that the outcomes can't be perfectly predicted.

Remember, life is the journey, not the destination. Whatever path we choose, there will be some things that go surprisingly well, and we can be grateful for them; and some things that challenge us. Every time there is a challenge, there is an opportunity for growth. You've heard phrases like 'I've learnt more from my failures than my successes', or 'there's no such thing as failure, only feedback'. So, while a cock-up may feel bad at the time, within it lies a rich development opportunity. So be thankful and know that you'll never meet a strong person that's had an easy past.

Celebrate the troubles. And know that there is no wrong path – they either lead to great outcomes, or great lessons, or perhaps both. Sometimes the best things in life arise from moments that originally felt 'bad'.

Reflect & Write: How about you? Have you ever come through something difficult and, on reflection, consider it to be one of the best things that ever happened? What was it?

CHAPTER 9
PANIC

What Is a Panic Attack?

Panic attacks are a type of fear response. They're an exaggeration of the body's normal response to danger, stress or excitement. If you've never suffered from one, I've heard them described beautifully as the feeling you get when you've rocked back on a chair slightly too far, and it's about to fall – except the pounding feeling in your chest doesn't pass quickly, and you have no idea why it started.

In anxiety attacks, you may feel fearful, apprehensive, feel your heart racing or feel short of breath, but it's very short-lived, and when the stressor goes away, the anxiety attack dissipates. Panic attacks, on the other hand, don't come in reaction to a stressor; they're unprovoked and unpredictable.

Attacks Always Pass

Panic attacks aren't dangerous despite how they feel in the moment. You can't faint since your high heart rate is raising rather than lowering your blood pressure (the cause of passing out), and unless the intense pain in your chest literally floors you, it's not a heart attack. If there is a shortness of breath, the mix of oxygen and carbon dioxide in the bloodstream is out of proportion, which can lead to a feeling of light-headedness but can't lead to suffocation, as the breath will always, eventually, return to normal. Most panic attacks last between five and 20 minutes, with symptoms peaking within 10 minutes, and then they pass. Always.

If some symptoms last longer then it's likely that there is an underlying cause of anxiety, and while this book may help you, it may be helpful for you to seek additional support from your doctor or a counsellor.

Here are some techniques that can both stave off a panic attack and help ease one on its way if it arrives.

Breath Awareness

Place your right hand high on your chest. Place your left hand on your belly. Breathe normally and focus your attention on the movement of your hands. Set a timer on your phone and give a full minute of pure awareness to the motion without attempting to change it in any way.

How do you feel now? If you started with a calm state of

mind, it's likely that you now feel very relaxed. The internal chatter of the mind has subsided, you feel at peace and yet still alert.

The breath is always with you and has been since birth. Practising 'breath awareness' is one of the most useful techniques for maintaining balance and a sense of perspective. To survive any moment, all that is required is air in your lungs, and there it is – always, just there!

When you find anxious thoughts arising, a great habit to foster is to turn your attention to the movement of the breath for 60 seconds. And even better, make breath awareness a daily habit whether you're feeling anxious or not – the practice will make it easier when you need it most.

The fact that you have the only thing that is truly necessary for life right here is reassuring and will instantly reduce all other stress symptoms. Get into the routine of practising this when you sense the first feelings of unease, and you'll reduce the frequency of falling into the full throes of panic.

Mindfulness

Mindfulness is the psychological process of bringing your attention to experiences happening in the present moment. If your internal experiences are uncomfortable, the practice can be unhelpful as it can accentuate the feeling of discomfort, so from a stress-relieving perspective, it's important to tune into what you can experience about the external world.

Let's give this a go right now. Start by tuning into your sense of sound. Set a timer for 60 seconds, and then get comfortable. Close your eyes (to remove visual distractions), and simply notice all the sounds in your environment, ensuring that you're gathering the data from noises both near and far.

How was that?

For me, sound works best. For others, one of the other senses may be more powerful. Try a different way of seeing: Bring both arms straight out in front of you at eye level, with your hands clenched, knuckles touching, and your thumbs sticking straight up. Close one eye and look directly through the gap between your thumbs, bringing your focus onto whatever falls within the narrow field of view.

Really concentrate on it, noticing the colour, texture, and how light falls on it. You are experiencing 'foveal vision', and it is associated with deep concentration. Now, keeping both thumbs in your field of view, and at eye level, move your hands slowly apart until they are stretched out sideways. Check that both thumbs are still in your field of view by giving them a little wiggle.

You are now experiencing something called 'peripheral vision'. Lower your arms but relax the muscles around your eyes and allow everything in your field of view to be in your visual awareness. When your eyes focus or get naturally drawn to something specific, simply invite everything else back into your awareness.

Sit calmly in this state for as long as you like. Returning, when distracted, to the whole picture.

How was that? How are you feeling now? Has your breathing slowed, has your mind chatter ceased? Are you feeling calmer, yet alert? This is the effect of mindfulness, and now you know how to get into peripheral vision you don't need to do the whole arm-raising thing, it's possible to shift your state simply by sitting with an expanded field of vision whenever you like.

A third method is to bring attention to what you are touching. No need to close your eyes this time, or raise your arms, you can do this anywhere anytime without anyone else knowing you're doing it!

Wherever your body makes contact with something, place your attention on it. In detail. Just one touchpoint at a time and when you feel you have noticed everything there is to notice about how it physically feels, then move to touch-point number two. Once you have gone around each touchpoint, return to whichever one now calls for your attention and notice what has changed in your perception since you last gave it your full attention.

Whichever method you use, you are experiencing mindfulness, and it's proven to reduce anxiety. Like all skills, mindfulness requires practice, and it's better to practice when things aren't too difficult rather than test your novice technique in the crucible of stress. Try one technique per day. Set a time when you'll do it – perhaps when you are commuting, or at the bus stop, or right before you turn on the computer. You choose how you will develop it as a positive habit.

Reflect & Write: How can you bring brief moments of pausing into your daily routine? Which mindfulness practice would you like to experiment with?

CHAPTER 10
GRIT

Dig In

IQ doesn't perfectly correlate to school grades. Research by popular science author Angela Duckworth found that 'the biggest predictor of success isn't IQ, it is grit.' It turns out that trying really hard matters too! So I was super happy when my son started primary school, and within a fortnight was enthusiastically talking about one of the school mottos (and the foundation of grit): 'We Persevere.'

Interestingly, grit isn't correlated to talent. Duckworth relates grit to the growth mindset – the ability to learn isn't fixed. For individuals with a growth mindset, failure isn't a permanent condition; they know the brain grows in response to challenges. As you have worked through the exercises in the previous sections, you have grown your grit, and therefore statistically speaking, you are more likely to be successful than before you picked up this book. Sometimes you just have to dig in, the treasure is buried deep – perseverance is required.

How Gritty Are You?

Head on over to AngelaDuckworth.com for a 10-question test which gives you a personal grit score, and if you don't have access to the Internet right now simply ponder this statement:

'I finish whatever I begin.'

The degree to which you agree with the statement is likely to be similar to the degree to which you have grit.

Low grit ratings mean that you've got space to grow and can expect greater success if you're willing to bring a growth mindset to them. Let's start this process by taking a look at how you feel about setbacks.

Bounce-back-ability

When you simply see results, it may appear that success comes easily to some people. But the reality is that on most occasions when you look more deeply, the difference between success and failure is sheer persistence.

Success

Success

WHAT PEOPLE THINK
IT LOOKS LIKE

WHAT IT REALLY
LOOKS LIKE

Reflect & Write: Reflecting on your life, what success have you really had to work for? Select a project, something that took some time, went through some ups and downs, and that you're genuinely proud of. Draw the axis of a graph with time on the x-axis and difficulty on the y-axis. Now plot your project along the timeline – noticing the ups and downs of how it felt along the way.

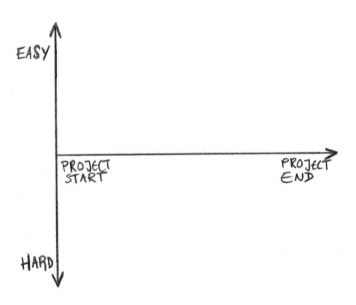

When you hit a trough, and things got tough, how did you keep going? If your project fits almost entirely below the line – and was pretty much hard from start to finish, then how did you keep going? Why didn't you quit?

Reflect & Write: When things got tough, how did you keep going?

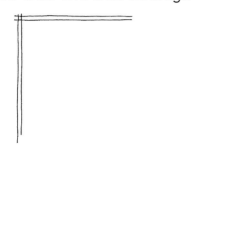

This project you've plotted is something that you are really proud of. On reflection, it's one of your life highlights. If it had been easy all the time, would you be as proud? Would it have been a life highlight? If you didn't have to push through challenges, would you be genuinely proud of anything?

Everything you do that matters will have ups and downs, and sometimes the 'ups' only come after the project ends and you can reflect with pride about how you overcame the 'downs'. How much you are prepared to suffer to achieve the goal depends on how much you care about the outcome.

When setting goals it's essential to make sure they really do matter to you. In the book *OWN LIFE WITH PURPOSE*, we take a deep dive into this topic to make sure your personal life dreams are turned into richly powerful goals that sustain you through the downs. To achieve your goal, you will suffer. This is essential for growth, and for the deep sense of achievement that comes when you hit the finish line.

Giving Up vs Letting Go

If I give up it means I'm throwing in the towel of defeat, my perseverance is gone, and I am disappointed. This is entirely different from those things I choose to let go of. Letting go means I free myself from something that is not important enough to continue striving for.

In the past, you may have given yourself a hard time for quitting something when, in reality, you were freeing yourself. At one time, I would always finish a book that I started reading; until I acknowledged that some books weren't worth the effort. I freed myself, and now I read more good books because I am happy to let go of the bad ones. If you're carrying unhelpful baggage, then to fly, you have to throw it overboard. The bags that you throw out, if you choose them carefully, aren't important to your life success but they are holding you back. So, let them go. They are not failures, but they may be causing your life to fail.

Reflect & Write: It's probably also true that sometimes you gave up because you lacked grit. Let's get examples of each: Write down five challenges you were right to let go of, and then five challenges you gave up on.

It may now feel better to re-label some things as 'letting go', and this is critical to achieving the big stuff (we return to this topic when we look at time management in *OWN LIFE WITH PURPOSE*).

Reflect & Write: When you look at the other list, the list of things that you gave up on, how does it feel?

Reflect & Write: Reflecting on the five (or more) scenarios where you've given up, list all the reasons why, in the past, you have quit.

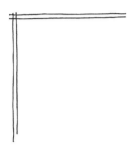

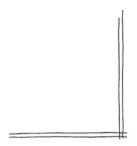

Applying a Growth Mindset

Run through the list and see where accountability lies. If other more important priorities came along then it's not 'quitting', it's 'letting go', and is good prioritization, so you can cross those off the list. If you've written something that is within your control (e.g. procrastination, fear of failure, etc.) then great, we'll take action on those things next. If something on your list is due to something entirely outside your sphere of control (e.g. legislation change made it illegal), then you can write those off as 'shit happens', the world isn't fair.

But if you regularly seem to say, 'Why does it always happen to me?' then check whether you are taking appropriate accountability for your own life or looking externally to divert blame. Take a look at anything on your list that isn't entirely in your control, but you could have influence over (e.g. teammates). If you wrote, 'I quit because my boss doesn't like me', or 'my teammate didn't pull their weight', then you are externalising all the blame, and this won't help you in the future when facing similar challenges. So, rewrite anything where you have influence so that you can then choose a course of action. For example, 'I quit because I was unable to manage my emotional responses towards certain behaviours of my boss', or 'I quit because I wasn't able to inspire and motivate my teammates effectively'. The rewording may feel subtle, but it fundamentally shifts your position from victim to empowered.

In the past, these things have caused you to quit. But they don't have to in the future because the brain grows through challenge. You can be more capable of pushing through the challenges in the future, so let's put a 'yet' into a sentence and then you can give yourself some advice for the future.

Here's an example:

I quit because other team members weren't pulling their weight. I'm not able to motivate lazy people... yet.

When an important goal is blocked by lazy people in the future, the advice I have for myself is to: a) find the right words to be gently straight with them about how I feel about their work ethic, and/or b) try to find out what is getting in their way and therefore stand in their shoes a little better; and/or c) reallocate the work and take the person off the project; and/or d) accept that I have to step in more (suck it up because the world isn't fair).

Reflect & Write: Over to you. Take three of the most common reasons why you've quit in the past. Write it as a growth mindset statement (i.e. it includes the word 'yet'), and then give yourself some advice for the future.

Perfectionism

I sometimes hear people say, 'I'm a perfectionist', and they're guiltily proud of this trait. But little gets in the way of happiness or progress more than an expectation of perfection. It's a common reason to quit something. But we don't have to ditch the quest for perfection, we simply need to reframe the level at which it is applied. When it's applied at the micro-level, where every little thing needs to be perfectly completed, then it's stifling and causes the big picture to be a million miles from perfection.

So, we need to flip things. What we really seek is the perfect big picture, which means accepting that everything within the picture has to be good enough.

For example, when I visualize my perfect life it includes authoring best-selling self-help books; facilitating large training events; training for endurance sports events; being very present in my kids' everyday lives; long frequent conversations with my wife; and travelling the world. Each element needs to be present in the big picture, and each needs to be 'right-sized' to allow space for all the other elements to fit.

At this level, it's now easy to see that perfection actually means 'the right size for the total composition', and not 'maximized'. In practice, this means that my sports training is 'right-sized' to get me to the start and finish line of endurance events, but not onto the podium, since training to that level would squash all the other elements and make the big picture pretty ugly.

At a micro-level, I could be self-critical that I'm not achieving my sporting potential, yet by stepping back and seeing the entirety of life, I can see that I am achieving my life potential. You sometimes have to let go of damaging expectations in one area to paint the full picture.

What has this got to do with resilience? It's about expectation setting. Too many of us give ourselves a hard time because we're not living up to what perfection looks like in our imagination, and so we quit.

Reflect & Write: How about you? In what areas of your life are you setting yourself an unrealistically high expectation?

Reframing Failure

People with a fixed mindset see success or failure as evidence that someone is talented or not, and therefore failure should be avoided. This causes them to take the safe options, stay in the comfort zone, and feel good about repeatedly doing the same things well. They are stuck. To grow means putting yourself into new situations where, by definition, you have less experience. Measured against those things you have already mastered, the new things you try will feel awkward, and great results will be less easy to come by. Measured in this way, failure is inevitable. The growth mindset celebrates effort above talent. Failure is simply feedback.

Here's a nice way to reframe the goal of any activity so that you are guaranteed to be 100 per cent successful all of the time: Whatever you are doing, the goal is to learn as much as possible so the next time you do it, you do it better.

If the activity achieves the desired outcome, what did you do that made it successful? And what could you do to make it more successful? If it failed, what have you learnt that would increase the chance of success next time?

Reflect & Write: Consider something that you failed at recently. What have you learnt about yourself, others, or the environment?

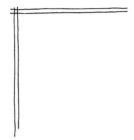

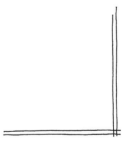

There genuinely is no such thing as failure as long as you have a growth mindset, so when facing challenges, set yourself the goal to learn.

Habits for Success

There's no single silver bullet that leads to success; it's a meandering path of failure, lessons and grit. It takes a suite of skills that need practice. The techniques are all in the Own Life Collection; it's up to you to put them into action. What would make you more resilient to setbacks?

Here's a list, with their corresponding book:

- Believing I'm fine just the way I am. (*Own Life with Confidence*)
- Believing in myself. (*Own Life with Confidence*)
- Accepting that I can change and adopting a growth mindset. (*Own Life with Confidence*)
- Acknowledging and managing shifting emotions. (*Own Life with Courage*)
- Handling setbacks and inner critic. (*Own Life with Courage*)
- A strong sense of purpose, razor-sharp goals and good planning. (*Own Life with Purpose*)
- Taking care of the most precious commodity, time. (*Own Life with Purpose*)
- Maintaining positive mental, physical and emotional energy. (*Own Life with Purpose*)
- Nurturing a caring support network. (*Own Life with Trust*)

CHAPTER 11
CONCLUDING THOUGHTS

Fear is a natural human instinct that keeps you safe. However, sometimes its overprotective nature holds you back. By acknowledging the fear, and consistently facing into gently increasing doses of it, you develop a greater capacity to quieten the limiting beliefs you hold and begin to say hello to the voice that says, 'I can handle anything.'

The journey to success isn't a straight line; you will have setbacks. By combining grit with a growth mindset, failure can be turned into a rich lesson that brings you closer to your goals.

When El Davo first draws an illustration, he's super disappointed. He's not an accomplished speed-drawer (yet!). In his pencil case, he carries five different kinds of erasers and describes them as his favourite tool as they release him from the need for perfection. His bin overflows with failures, yet it's his grit and growth mindset that turns each one into a lesson and allows him to produce stunning art.

Take this as a metaphor for the journey ahead of you. It takes courage to put the first lines on a blank canvas, just as it takes courage for you to step into the uncertainty of experimenting with new behaviours. Of course you will make mistakes, it's guaranteed. So does El Davo. His erased pencil marks help to guide a new, more confident mark. It's this constant interplay between laying down a mark and then finding an improved one that is the key to his success. And it's the key to yours too.

EMOTIONAL INTELLIGENCE

IQ is Nothing Without EQ

We've all experienced times when our emotions have got in the way of our thinking, but we might not realize they are also the key to thinking. We literally can't make decisions without making use of emotion.

How smartly we use our emotions is measured by our emotional intelligence (often referred to as the emotional quotient, or EQ), and includes:

- How well we know and accept ourselves for who we truly are.
- The ability to be aware of and manage our emotional state.
- Having empathy to develop positive relationships.
- Being grounded in the realities of life, while having aspirations for the future.

Most people first heard the term 'emotional intelligence' around 1995 with the publication of Daniel Goleman's best-selling book, *Emotional Intelligence, Why it Can Matter*

More Than IQ. He laid out the case that EQ is the best predictor for life success. No matter how you wish to define success!

Non-profit organisation Six Seconds examined 75,000 individuals across 126 countries, and not only concluded that success and EQ are linked, but also that, 'EQ has twice the power of IQ to predict someone's performance'.

Because 'success' can mean different things to different people, Six Seconds cleverly used an average of four broad and balanced variables (effectiveness, relationships, wellbeing, and quality of life) to come to an 'average success' score. They agree with Goleman – EQ really is the best predictor of life success.

The extent to which you have emotional intelligence is broadly related to your upbringing, but thankfully this doesn't mean that your success is pre-determined, because unlike IQ, which is generally accepted to be fixed after the teenage years, emotional intelligence can be developed throughout life. And the best thing? You've been developing it since the first page of this book.

Emotional Intelligence isn't another new topic we're covering here in the epilogue. Instead, it is simply the perfect way to pull together the strands of everything you have already done and give it a single, simple, powerful label.

How Much Do I Have?

There is no global standardized test for EQ, and you will find many different versions available online – some of which are free. But you've already taken a test that is highly likely to correlate with any online EQ assessment that you can take. It is right back at the start of the book, on page 2.

Let's pause again to step back from the details of life,

and check-in. Well done for choosing to invest some time in yourself and pat yourself on the back for persevering to the end of the book – many of the self-reflection questions I posed are quite challenging.

Reflect & Write: Having worked through *OWN LIFE WITH COURAGE* I will…

Now let's get an up-to-date measure of how much you are owning life. Decide to what extent you agree or disagree with each of the following statements, and colour in the corresponding box in the chart that follows.

1. I know and accept myself for who I am
2. I believe I can become good at anything I choose to put my mind to
3. I maintain a positive emotional state of mind regardless of what is going on around me
4. I push through fear to accomplish things that are uncomfortable
5. What I do is aligned to a deeply held sense of purpose
6. I make the most of life by using my time wisely
7. I am like a battery, always full of energy and ready to go
8. I enjoy trusting, respectful relationships with everyone in my life

	STRONGLY DISAGREE	DISAGREE	NEUTRAL	AGREE	STRONGLY AGREE
1	☐	☐	☐	☐	☐
2.	☐	☐	☐	☐	☐
3.	☐	☐	☐	☐	☐
4.	☐	☐	☐	☐	☐
5.	☐	☐	☐	☐	☐
6.	☐	☐	☐	☐	☐
7.	☐	☐	☐	☐	☐
8.	☐	☐	☐	☐	☐

To get a crude metric that you can track over time, use the following scoring system. For every statement where you responded with Strongly Agree score 12.5, Agree = 10, Neutral = 5, Disagree = 2, and Strongly Disagree = 0. Add up the total points to get your Own Life percentage.

Remember that EQ is something you can work to develop. Wherever your scores are now, they can shift upwards provided you believe they can, and you are prepared to put in the (sometimes uncomfortable) effort.

Growing EQ

The self-assessment above gives you some insight into your relative strengths and weaknesses relating to emotional intelligence, but it doesn't enhance it. Enhancing it requires action. If you noticed your scores are higher than when you started the book, it's likely because you have experimented with some new actions. If you have got this far and haven't seen a shift in EQ, it's because you now have cognitive intelligence (you've read about what makes a difference) without the corresponding experiential lessons that are required to shift your life.

The question for you now is, to what depth did you choose to invest in yourself? I've been working in emotional intelligence for about a decade, and I constantly find I have new things to work on to improve myself. Writing this book has led to another layer of questions, and therefore another layer of insights about myself.

Nobody has perfect EQ. Therefore, development in this area is never 'done'. Having said that, it's not a subject that requires endless research. All the topics you need to cover are included in the Own Life Collection. The key isn't to make it an academic subject, read once and set aside, but a practical one.

Whatever the specific topic, the learning cycle is simple:

1. Reflect on where you are now.
2. Imagine where you'd like to be in the future.
3. Determine an action that will take you forwards.
4. Have the courage to undertake the action.
5. Reflect on the outcome of the action
6. Back to step number 1, and repeat, repeat, repeat.

Reflect & Write: Taking a look at your scores on the self-assessment. Which two statements would you most like to put under the spotlight of development over the next six months?

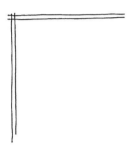

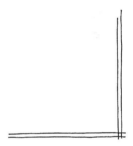

If you're ready to continue your OWN LIFE journey, where do you want to focus next?

OWN LIFE WITH CONFIDENCE:
How to grow into the best version of yourself
OWN LIFE WITH PURPOSE:
How to engineer a lifestyle that fulfils your dreams
OWN LIFE WITH TRUST:
How to develop positive relationships

Congratulations on choosing to develop yourself. If this becomes a lifelong habit I guarantee you a wonderful life, and I wish you the very best of luck with it.

PART 3
DAILY JOURNAL

DATE

THINGS I AM GRATEFUL FOR

1.
2.
3.

WHAT I WILL DO TO MAKE TODAY GREAT

1.
2.
3.

DAILY AFFIRMATION

I AM...

_____

AMAZING THINGS THAT HAPPENED TODAY

1.
2.
3.

HOW COULD I HAVE MADE TODAY BETTER?

DATE

THINGS I AM GRATEFUL FOR

1.
2.
3.

WHAT I WILL DO TO MAKE TODAY GREAT

1.
2.
3.

DAILY AFFIRMATION

I AM...

AMAZING THINGS THAT HAPPENED TODAY

1.
2.
3.

HOW COULD I HAVE MADE TODAY BETTER?

DATE

THINGS I AM GRATEFUL FOR

1.
2.
3.

WHAT I WILL DO TO MAKE TODAY GREAT

1.
2.
3.

DAILY AFFIRMATION

I AM...

_____

AMAZING THINGS THAT HAPPENED TODAY

1.
2.
3.

HOW COULD I HAVE MADE TODAY BETTER?

DATE

THINGS I AM GRATEFUL FOR

1.
2.
3.

WHAT I WILL DO TO MAKE TODAY GREAT

1.
2.
3.

DAILY AFFIRMATION

I AM...

_____

AMAZING THINGS THAT HAPPENED TODAY
1.
2.
3.

HOW COULD I HAVE MADE TODAY BETTER?

DATE

THINGS I AM GRATEFUL FOR

1.
2.
3.

WHAT I WILL DO TO MAKE TODAY GREAT

1.
2.
3.

DAILY AFFIRMATION

I AM...

AMAZING THINGS THAT HAPPENED TODAY

1.
2.
3.

HOW COULD I HAVE MADE TODAY BETTER?

DATE

THINGS I AM GRATEFUL FOR

1.
2.
3.

WHAT I WILL DO TO MAKE TODAY GREAT

1.
2.
3.

DAILY AFFIRMATION

I AM...

_____

AMAZING THINGS THAT HAPPENED TODAY

1.
2.
3.

HOW COULD I HAVE MADE TODAY BETTER?

DATE

THINGS I AM GRATEFUL FOR

1.
2.
3.

WHAT I WILL DO TO MAKE TODAY GREAT

1.
2.
3.

DAILY AFFIRMATION

I AM...

_____

AMAZING THINGS THAT HAPPENED TODAY
1.
2.
3.

HOW COULD I HAVE MADE TODAY BETTER?

DATE

THINGS I AM GRATEFUL FOR

1.
2.
3.

WHAT I WILL DO TO MAKE TODAY GREAT

1.
2.
3.

DAILY AFFIRMATION

I AM...

AMAZING THINGS THAT HAPPENED TODAY

1.
2.
3.

HOW COULD I HAVE MADE TODAY BETTER?

DATE

THINGS I AM GRATEFUL FOR

1.
2.
3.

WHAT I WILL DO TO MAKE TODAY GREAT

1.
2.
3.

DAILY AFFIRMATION

I AM...

AMAZING THINGS THAT HAPPENED TODAY

1.
2.
3.

HOW COULD I HAVE MADE TODAY BETTER?

DATE

THINGS I AM GRATEFUL FOR

1.
2.
3.

WHAT I WILL DO TO MAKE TODAY GREAT

1.
2.
3.

DAILY AFFIRMATION

I AM...

_____

AMAZING THINGS THAT HAPPENED TODAY

1.
2.
3.

HOW COULD I HAVE MADE TODAY BETTER?

DATE

THINGS I AM GRATEFUL FOR

1.
2.
3.

WHAT I WILL DO TO MAKE TODAY GREAT

1.
2.
3.

DAILY AFFIRMATION

I AM...

_____

AMAZING THINGS THAT HAPPENED TODAY

1.
2.
3.

HOW COULD I HAVE MADE TODAY BETTER?

DATE

THINGS I AM GRATEFUL FOR

1.
2.
3.

WHAT I WILL DO TO MAKE TODAY GREAT

1.
2.
3.

DAILY AFFIRMATION

I AM...

_____

AMAZING THINGS THAT HAPPENED TODAY
1.
2.
3.

HOW COULD I HAVE MADE TODAY BETTER?

DATE

THINGS I AM GRATEFUL FOR

1.
2.
3.

WHAT I WILL DO TO MAKE TODAY GREAT

1.
2.
3.

DAILY AFFIRMATION

I AM...

_____

AMAZING THINGS THAT HAPPENED TODAY
1.
2.
3.

HOW COULD I HAVE MADE TODAY BETTER?

DATE

THINGS I AM GRATEFUL FOR

1.
2.
3.

WHAT I WILL DO TO MAKE TODAY GREAT

1.
2.
3.

DAILY AFFIRMATION

I AM...

_____

AMAZING THINGS THAT HAPPENED TODAY

1.
2.
3.

HOW COULD I HAVE MADE TODAY BETTER?

DATE

THINGS I AM GRATEFUL FOR

1.
2.
3.

WHAT I WILL DO TO MAKE TODAY GREAT

1.
2.
3.

DAILY AFFIRMATION

I AM...

_____

AMAZING THINGS THAT HAPPENED TODAY
1.
2.
3.

HOW COULD I HAVE MADE TODAY BETTER?

DATE

THINGS I AM GRATEFUL FOR

1.
2.
3.

WHAT I WILL DO TO MAKE TODAY GREAT

1.
2.
3.

DAILY AFFIRMATION

I AM...

_____

AMAZING THINGS THAT HAPPENED TODAY

1.
2.
3.

HOW COULD I HAVE MADE TODAY BETTER?

DATE

THINGS I AM GRATEFUL FOR

1.
2.
3.

WHAT I WILL DO TO MAKE TODAY GREAT

1.
2.
3.

DAILY AFFIRMATION

I AM...

AMAZING THINGS THAT HAPPENED TODAY

1.
2.
3.

HOW COULD I HAVE MADE TODAY BETTER?

DATE

THINGS I AM GRATEFUL FOR

1.
2.
3.

WHAT I WILL DO TO MAKE TODAY GREAT

1.
2.
3.

DAILY AFFIRMATION

I AM...

_____

AMAZING THINGS THAT HAPPENED TODAY

1.
2.
3.

HOW COULD I HAVE MADE TODAY BETTER?

DATE

THINGS I AM GRATEFUL FOR

1.
2.
3.

WHAT I WILL DO TO MAKE TODAY GREAT

1.
2.
3.

DAILY AFFIRMATION

I AM...

AMAZING THINGS THAT HAPPENED TODAY
1.
2.
3.

HOW COULD I HAVE MADE TODAY BETTER?

DATE

THINGS I AM GRATEFUL FOR

1.
2.
3.

WHAT I WILL DO TO MAKE TODAY GREAT

1.
2.
3.

DAILY AFFIRMATION

I AM...

_____

AMAZING THINGS THAT HAPPENED TODAY
1.
2.
3.

HOW COULD I HAVE MADE TODAY BETTER?

THINGS I AM GRATEFUL FOR

1.
2.
3.

WHAT I WILL DO TO MAKE TODAY GREAT

1.
2.
3.

DAILY AFFIRMATION

I AM...

_____

AMAZING THINGS THAT HAPPENED TODAY
1.
2.
3.

HOW COULD I HAVE MADE TODAY BETTER?

DATE

THINGS I AM GRATEFUL FOR

1.
2.
3.

WHAT I WILL DO TO MAKE TODAY GREAT

1.
2.
3.

DAILY AFFIRMATION

I AM...

AMAZING THINGS THAT HAPPENED TODAY

1.
2.
3.

HOW COULD I HAVE MADE TODAY BETTER?

DATE

THINGS I AM GRATEFUL FOR

1.
2.
3.

WHAT I WILL DO TO MAKE TODAY GREAT

1.
2.
3.

DAILY AFFIRMATION

I AM...

AMAZING THINGS THAT HAPPENED TODAY
1.
2.
3.

HOW COULD I HAVE MADE TODAY BETTER?

DATE

THINGS I AM GRATEFUL FOR

1.
2.
3.

WHAT I WILL DO TO MAKE TODAY GREAT

1.
2.
3.

DAILY AFFIRMATION

I AM...

AMAZING THINGS THAT HAPPENED TODAY

1.
2.
3.

HOW COULD I HAVE MADE TODAY BETTER?

DATE

THINGS I AM GRATEFUL FOR

1.
2.
3.

WHAT I WILL DO TO MAKE TODAY GREAT

1.
2.
3.

DAILY AFFIRMATION

I AM...

AMAZING THINGS THAT HAPPENED TODAY

1.
2.
3.

HOW COULD I HAVE MADE TODAY BETTER?

DATE

THINGS I AM GRATEFUL FOR

1.
2.
3.

WHAT I WILL DO TO MAKE TODAY GREAT

1.
2.
3.

DAILY AFFIRMATION

I AM...

_____

AMAZING THINGS THAT HAPPENED TODAY

1.
2.
3.

HOW COULD I HAVE MADE TODAY BETTER?

DATE

THINGS I AM GRATEFUL FOR

1.
2.
3.

WHAT I WILL DO TO MAKE TODAY GREAT

1.
2.
3.

DAILY AFFIRMATION

I AM...

_____

AMAZING THINGS THAT HAPPENED TODAY
1.
2.
3.

HOW COULD I HAVE MADE TODAY BETTER?

DATE

THINGS I AM GRATEFUL FOR

1.
2.
3.

WHAT I WILL DO TO MAKE TODAY GREAT

1.
2.
3.

DAILY AFFIRMATION

I AM...

_____

AMAZING THINGS THAT HAPPENED TODAY
1.
2.
3.

HOW COULD I HAVE MADE TODAY BETTER?

DATE

THINGS I AM GRATEFUL FOR

1.

2.

3.

WHAT I WILL DO TO MAKE TODAY GREAT

1.

2.

3.

DAILY AFFIRMATION

I AM...

_____

AMAZING THINGS THAT HAPPENED TODAY

1.

2.

3.

HOW COULD I HAVE MADE TODAY BETTER?

DATE

THINGS I AM GRATEFUL FOR

1.
2.
3.

WHAT I WILL DO TO MAKE TODAY GREAT

1.
2.
3.

DAILY AFFIRMATION

I AM...

_____

AMAZING THINGS THAT HAPPENED TODAY

1.
2.
3.

HOW COULD I HAVE MADE TODAY BETTER?

DEAR READER...

The very best thing about what I do is when I get to see people grow into their own skin and radiate a comfortable ease that only comes with being their wonderful authentic self. The magic is multiplied when I get to be a witness (and occasional mentor) as they continue their life journey. I would love to add you to the community of people I know who are actively working on improving themselves.

From time-to-time I share stories of my journey. The successes and the struggles. I also test new material and ask for guidance from my readers on what would be most helpful in the future. If you'd like to be a part of the Own Life community go to www.ownlife.me/connect

And... you can make a big difference to me right away.

Reviews are the most powerful way for an independent publisher like myself to help new readers find my books. And reviews are the most trusted source when new readers are choosing how to spend their money.

Honest reviews of my books help to nourish the entire system. If you've enjoyed this book, I would be super-appreciative if you could spend just five minutes leaving a review (which can be as brief as you like).

I really hope that I've been able to help you on your Own Life journey.

With big thanks,

todd@ownlife.me

ABOUT THE AUTHOR

Todd Eden's sole mission in life is to bring out the best in people. It wasn't always this way! Right through childhood and through his first couple of careers, he was insatiably competitive – great at bringing out his personal best and achieving results, but not always with great consideration for everyone around him.

Thankfully he married someone who simply oozes kindness. The resulting upgrade, Todd version 2.0, retains his authentic ambition to win at life but now defines winning as 'bringing out the best in others'.

This mission has taken him around the world working with multi-national companies; into the lecture theatres of a third of the UK's universities; and deep into the lives of his personal coaching clients.

He remains a passionate student of self-development and has been living and breathing it daily for decades. At live events he enjoys bringing his unique combination of profound life shifting moments with belly laugh humour to thousands of people. It's his wish that this book brings out the best in many thousands more.

Connect with Todd at www.ownlife.me/connect

ABOUT THE ILLUSTRATOR

From a young age, El Davo enjoyed art, and from seeing other people's reactions, he learned he had a talent. He attributes some of this to being curious and observational of his surroundings – or a daydreamer as others might put it. Those around him saw the need to nurture this talent well before he was aware of it himself.

He was lucky enough that his older sister was an artist, always there to offer invaluable support and encouragement when he was growing up. She lived in London at the time and regularly took him around the city to different galleries, as well as showing him all the graffiti and street art hotspots. Later she convinced him to pursue an art education beyond sixth form and attend art college, and after that, university.

Initially, he never felt like he'd earned this talent, but nonetheless felt obliged to make the most of it. He constantly strives to improve, for both the buzz of exceeding his own expectations and the joy it brings others. He especially loves to hear of people inspired enough to get back into doing art themselves. He firmly believes there's a huge pool of untapped creative talent in society, stuck inside people who haven't had the support and encouragement he's been fortunate enough to receive.

Connect with El Davo at www.eldavo.co.uk or on Instagram @eldavooo

"I believe in myself. I know and accept myself for exactly who I am today and feel inspired by how I will grow into the future."

[You, 6 months from now]

How to Grow Into the Best Version of Yourself

Accept yourself for who you are today, with all the beautiful flaws, without judgement

Clearly see a future enhanced version of yourself that is still authentically you

Overcome resistance to change and keep the development journey rolling

"My inner world is a positive place even when the outside world has its ups and downs. I'm resilient to setbacks and have found courage to push through fears that used to hold me back."

[You, 6 months from now]

How to Thrive on the Emotional Rollercoaster of Life

Create a separation between external events and internal emotions

Reprogram the filters through which you experience the world

Dare to do what you dream by pushing through fear

"I know where I'm heading in life and am grounded enough to enjoy each passing moment. I dream big, set plans, and make them happen. It's a thrill to be alive."
[You, 6 months from now]

How to Engineer a Lifestyle that Fulfills your Dreams

Turn dreams, wishes and hopes into goals that feel tinglingly possible

Give focus to your most precious priorities as you become a blackbelt time master

Feel alive every day with energy habits that boost resilience

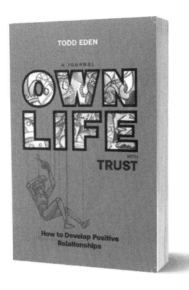

"From making a good first impression to repairing age-old broken relationships; from deepening my most loving friendships to navigating conflict, I build trust with others."
[You, 6 months from now]

How to Develop Positive Relationships

Reframe your attitude to conflict through an enhanced desire to see new perspectives

Respond with calm maturity when triggered by the behaviour of others

Unleash the simple magic of listening with wholehearted attention

ENDNOTES

1   Kashdan, T. and Biswas-Diener, R. (2015) The Upside of Your Darkside. New York: Plume.
2   Peters, S. (2012) The Chimp Paradox. London: Vermilion. Page 69.

INDEX

Printed in Great Britain
by Amazon